PEOPLE

Written by A. Langley & M. Butterfield

Illustrated by N. Young

GALLERY BOOKS
An Imprint of W. H. Smith Publishers Inc.
112 Madison Avenue
New York City 10016

ALL ABOUT PEOPLE

This book is all about different ways of life around the world. There are eight chapters, each one dealing with a different aspect of people's lives. In this chapter you can find out about the world's population. The other chapters are explained below.

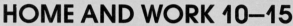

HOME AND WORK 10–15

This chapter is about the homes people live in and the places where they work. You can find out about shopping, too.

FAMILY LIFE 16–21

This section is about daily family life around the world, and also includes information on daily education and eating habits.

LANGUAGE/CUSTOMS 22–29

In this chapter there is information on languages, clothes, games, sports, and festivals around the world.

ART AND MUSIC 30–35

Every country has its own traditional art, music, and handicrafts. In this section you can find out about some of them.

RELIGION 36–39

There are many different religions around the world. In this section you can find out about the main religious groups.

POLITICS AND LAW 40–43

Most countries have a government to make the laws. This chapter is about different types of government.

FUTURE WORLD 44–45

You can find out how people's lives might change in this chapter, as new technology spreads around the world.

WHY THE DIFFERENCES?

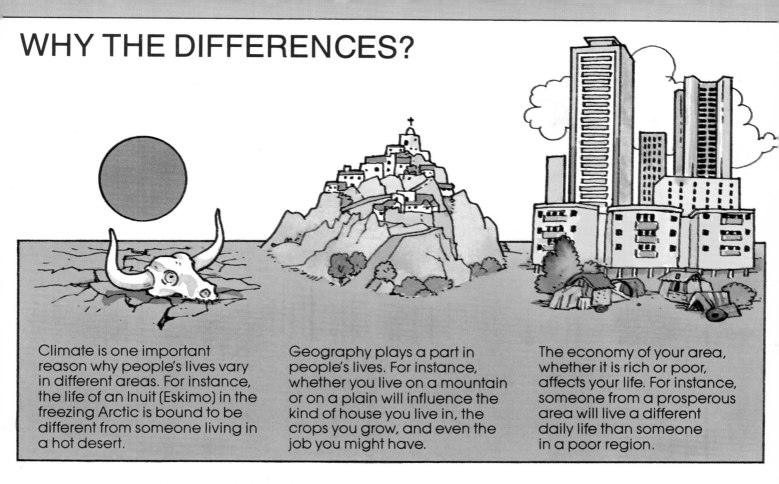

Climate is one important reason why people's lives vary in different areas. For instance, the life of an Inuit (Eskimo) in the freezing Arctic is bound to be different from someone living in a hot desert.

Geography plays a part in people's lives. For instance, whether you live on a mountain or on a plain will influence the kind of house you live in, the crops you grow, and even the job you might have.

The economy of your area, whether it is rich or poor, affects your life. For instance, someone from a prosperous area will live a different daily life than someone in a poor region.

DEVELOPED NATIONS

In areas such as North America, Europe, and Australasia, countries are usually wealthy. They have lots of industry and services, such as water, electricity, roads, and railroads.

In these countries there are usually lots of built-up cities and towns, with plenty of stores where people can buy the goods they need. Areas like this are often referred to as "developed countries."

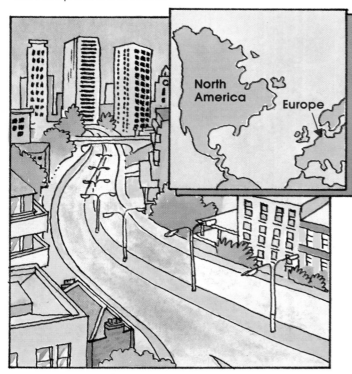

DEVELOPING NATIONS

In places such as Africa and Asia, many countries are still trying to organize their own industries and services. Areas like this are often referred to as "developing countries."

Although there are often large cities in developing countries, many people live in small communities, growing their own food, making the tools they need, and building their own homes from local materials.

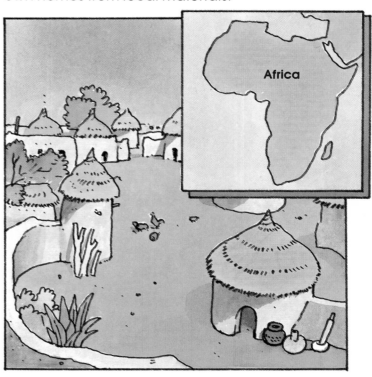

WORLD POPULATION

Population is the number of people who live in an area. The world's population is around 5 billion people, and it is estimated that about 150 people are born every minute, so the world's population increases by over 200,000 people per day! The map below shows how the numbers are spread out.

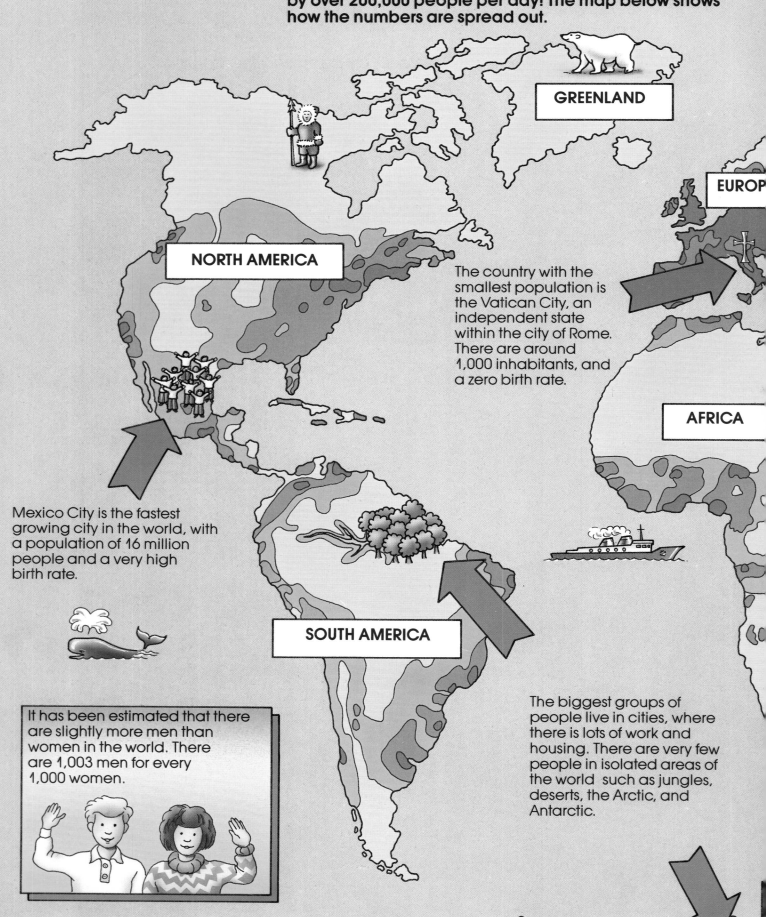

GREENLAND

EUROP

NORTH AMERICA

The country with the smallest population is the Vatican City, an independent state within the city of Rome. There are around 1,000 inhabitants, and a zero birth rate.

AFRICA

Mexico City is the fastest growing city in the world, with a population of 16 million people and a very high birth rate.

SOUTH AMERICA

It has been estimated that there are slightly more men than women in the world. There are 1,003 men for every 1,000 women.

The biggest groups of people live in cities, where there is lots of work and housing. There are very few people in isolated areas of the world such as jungles, deserts, the Arctic, and Antarctic.

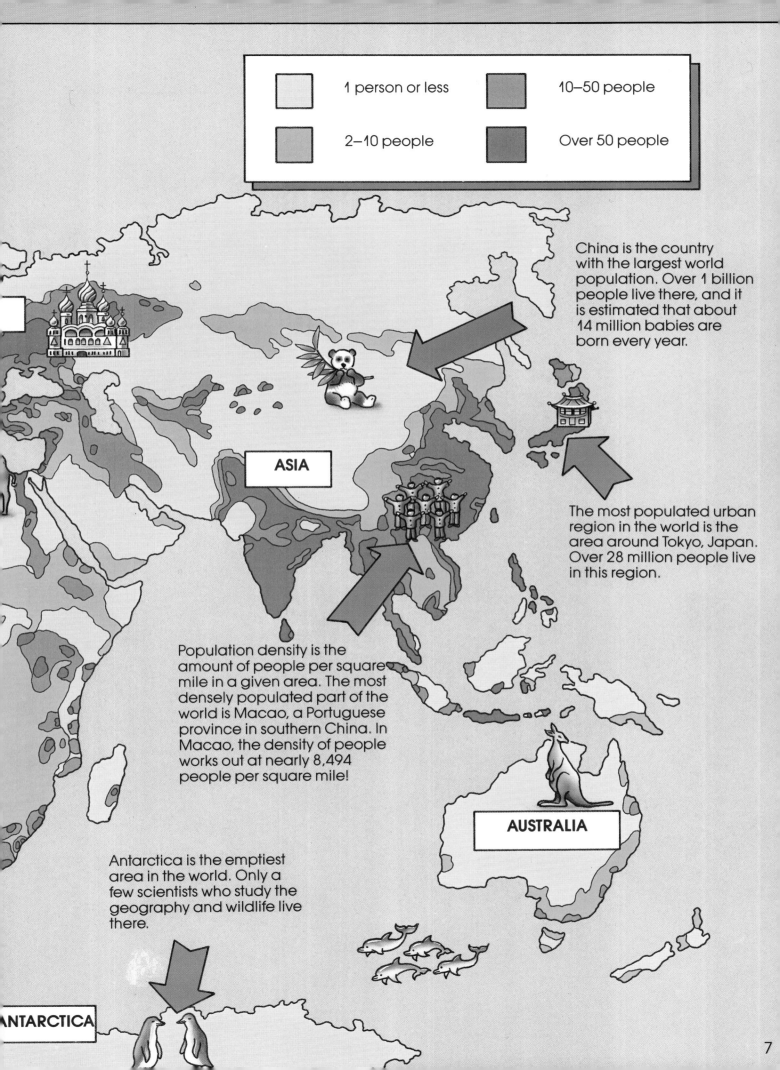

	1 person or less		10–50 people
	2–10 people		Over 50 people

China is the country with the largest world population. Over 1 billion people live there, and it is estimated that about 14 million babies are born every year.

ASIA

The most populated urban region in the world is the area around Tokyo, Japan. Over 28 million people live in this region.

Population density is the amount of people per square mile in a given area. The most densely populated part of the world is Macao, a Portuguese province in southern China. In Macao, the density of people works out at nearly 8,494 people per square mile!

AUSTRALIA

Antarctica is the emptiest area in the world. Only a few scientists who study the geography and wildlife live there.

ANTARCTICA

FILLING THE WORLD

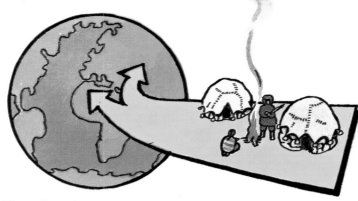

Scientists think that the first humans probably lived in central Africa over a million years ago. At this time most of the world was covered in ice, and only the area near the equator was warm enough for humans.

The climate gradually grew warmer and the ice began to melt. Humans began to settle further away; some went to North Africa and Europe, while others went to Asia. People learned to build shelters, light fires, and hunt for food.

During the Ice Age there was a land link between Siberia and Alaska. People traveled across this link from Europe, and colonized America. Eventually human beings settled on every continent except Antarctica.

By about 30,000 years ago, human settlements had spread right across Asia to the Pacific coast. Some people even built boats and landed on the northern shores of Australia. Today's Aborigines are their descendants.

TYPES OF PEOPLE

There are many types of people in the world, but they can be roughly divided into three main groups.

The Negroid people originate from Africa. Their dark skins help to protect them from the burning rays of the sun.

The Caucasoid people have pale skin in places with cold climates, and olive-colored skin in warm climates. The people of Europe, India, and the Arab lands are of Caucasoid origin.

Two out of every three people in the world are of Mongoloid origin. They tend to have straight, black hair and high cheekbones. Their eyelids have an extra fold. Most of the people who live in Asia are of Mongoloid origin.

WORLD PEOPLE FACTFINDER

The tallest people in the world are the Watusi of Rwanda in Africa. Many of them are nearly 7 feet tall. The smallest people in the world are the Baka of Zaire in Africa. Few of them grow taller than 5 feet.

People are now living longer than ever before. In 1950 the average world lifespan was 45.8 years. Today the average is 58.9 years. The people of Iceland have the highest world average at 76.7 years.

Many countries take their modern names from ancient tribal inhabitants. For instance, England is named after the ancient tribe of the Angles. France is named after the Franks, Denmark after the Danes, and Czechoslovakia after two different tribes — Czechs and Slovaks.

In 1900 there were about 1.6 billion people in the world. In 1950 there were about 2.5 billion. By 1989 that total had doubled to over 5 billion! That means that the world's population is now growing by about 76 million every year.

The earliest signs of human life are a set of footprints discovered in Tanzania, Africa. They were made over 3 million years ago by a group of manlike creatures walking across some volcanic ash. The ash later became hard and the footprints were preserved.

According to records, the oldest person who has ever lived was Shigechiyo Izumi of Japan. He was born in 1865 and died in 1986, at the age of 120 years and 237 days.

HOMES & WORK

The sort of homes people live in vary according to the places where they live. Their daily work lives vary, too. For instance, someone in Europe or America might work in a large factory, whereas someone in a remote African region is more likely to spend their time farming or hunting.

WHERE'S YOUR HOME?

Some settlements first developed in places where there was a good climate for crops.

Some settlements were first situated where there was plenty of material to build houses.

Many settlements were first founded in places where there was a water supply.

Sometimes settlements were built in places which were easy to defend against enemies.

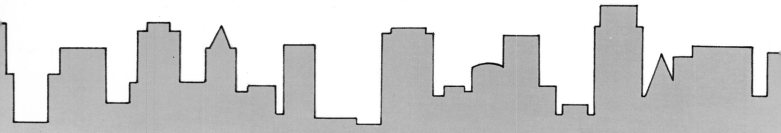

CITY LIVING

In cities there are lots of buildings crowded together. People tend to live in large apartment buildings because there is less room for individual housing.

One advantage of living in cities is that there are usually lots of services easily available, such as stores, hospitals, transportation, water, and electricity.

COUNTRY LIVING

In the countryside there is more room for houses. Individual homes and settlements tend to be much further apart from each other, with agricultural land in between.

Life in the countryside is quieter and less busy than city life, but there are often fewer services such as transportation and stores, and hospitals can be a long way away.

SPECIAL HOMES

In hot, dry places such as Africa, houses are sometimes built from mud mixed with straw to make it firmer. The sun bakes the thick mud walls hard, and they help to keep the heat of the sun out of the hut. Sometimes thatched roofs are added to keep off the rain during the monsoon season.

The picture on the right shows a much more complicated African hut, skilfully built from local materials.

The roof is constructed from bamboo poles, woven together and tied on to the house frame with wood bark straps. The thatching is made from straw.

African hut in Malawi.

Cave dwelling

People who live in caves are called "troglodytes." There are several troglodyte settlements still found in Middle Eastern regions of the world.

Bedouin tent

The Bedouins of the Arabian desert live in tents woven from goat hair. There is no furniture inside; instead there are rugs and cushions.

Village on stilts

In West African and Chinese fishing areas some villages are built on stilts embedded in the bottom of lakes. The only access is by boat.

Underground house

Recently there have been experiments in building underground houses, with windows in the roof to let in light.

PEOPLE AT WORK

All over the world people work in order to feed and clothe themselves. Some people spend their time hunting for food. Others grow food on farms or work to earn the money to buy food.

HUNTERS

There are still many hunting tribes in the world today. One example are the Waorani Indians of the Amazon.

The men of the Waorani tribe spend their days hunting monkeys and birds, using bows and arrows or long blowpipes which fire powerful poison-tipped darts.

Waorani hunters

Masai herdsmen

FARMERS

Many people spend their time farming. One example are the Masai of Kenya, who keep herds of cattle. Without this meat and milk the Masai would find it hard to survive.

Some farmers grow mainly crops. For instance, farmers in Southeast Asia grow rice, spending many hours each day in their flooded paddy fields, where the rice plants are grown.

The main food crops of the world are corn, wheat, rice, and vegetables.

The majority of farms in the world are small, with only a few animals and crops.

However, in places such as North America and Australia farms can be very large scale. Some Australian sheep farms cover more than a million acres, and farmers must use airplanes to inspect them.

CRAFTS

Persian rugmaking

Craft workers are people who make unique goods by hand, using skills such as pottery or weaving. One example is the making of Persian rugs in the Middle East. These are famous throughout the world for their beauty.

The weavers usually work at home, weaving on big wooden looms. Above the looms hang balls of wool in many different colors. They have been dyed using the natural colors from leaves, berries, and sometimes even insects.

MANUFACTURING

Many people work in factories, making all kinds of products. Nowadays a lot of hard factory work is done by machines, often computer-controlled. But the factories still need people to check that the machines are operating correctly.

In the U.S., cars are assembled in huge factories, where much of the heavy labor, such as welding and riveting, is done by robot-controlled machines. The U.S. produces more cars than any other country in the world.

WORKING FOR OTHERS

One of the most important ways of earning a living is by helping other people. For instance, fire fighters and police officers help protect homes and property, and teachers help people learn.

Doctors and nurses are important in every country. In many places they use the latest medicines and equipment, but in some countries ancient healing methods are still practiced. For example, in East Asia many doctors still treat their patients with herbs or the ancient art of acupuncture, which involves pricking parts of the body with tiny needles.

13

SHOPPING

Few people can grow or make everything they need. Most people must buy some food, clothing and other goods, and there is a huge variety of stores and markets all over the world.

In North America and Europe many people shop in large stores, sometimes in shopping centers. These are often built outside towns and must be reached by car.

The world's largest shopping center is the West Edmonton Mall, in Alberta, Canada. It covers 110 acres, and holds over 800 stores. It can handle half a million shoppers a week!

Floating market

The oldest type of store is the market, where local farmers, fishermen, and craftsmen bring their produce to sell. For example, in a village market in Nigeria you can buy such things as vegetables, fish, cloth, sugarcane, palm wine, nuts, and caged birds. The shoppers carry away their purchases balanced on their heads.

On the Caribbean island of Curaçao there is a floating market. Fishermen sail up and sell their catch from their boats.

The biggest market is the souq or bazaar in Aleppo, Syria. It covers an area of more than 9 miles.

In some countries, the stores come to the shoppers! For example, Indian butchers and fruit sellers take their wares from door to door.

Families living in remote settlements in the Australian Outback may be hundreds of miles from the nearest town. However, they can buy what they need from the "shopping train." It travels all over the Outback, stopping at each settlement so that the local people can stock up on supplies.

HOME AND WORK FACTFINDER

The country with the most doctors in the world is the USSR. There are 830,000 Russian doctors, one for every 300 people.

When an earthquake struck Peru in 1970, thousands of people lost their homes, but many were then given temporary plastic houses. These were made by blowing up large rubber balloons and covering the outside with quick-setting plastic. Once the plastic had set, the balloon was deflated and windows and doors were cut out.

A group of 21 huts near Nice, in France, are the oldest homes yet discovered. They date back over 400,000 years. Archeologists discovered that each house had a fireplace, which proves that they were almost certainly inhabited at one time.

The largest private home in the world is Biltmore House in North Carolina. It has over 250 rooms. The record for the most expensive house goes to the Hearst Ranch in California, built between 1922 and 1939. Even in those days the cost was over 30 million dollars!

The largest factory in the world is the Railroad Car and Tank Plant near Sverdlovsk in the USSR. It covers 204 acres of land, room for over 150 football fields.

Many Japanese people stay with the same company all their working lives. They often begin the day in offices or factories by doing exercises and singing the company song. As well as working together, the Japanese often relax together after work. Many Japanese even go on vacation with their workmates.

Overall, Saudi Arabian workers are the highest paid in the world, largely due to the country's income from oil. The average Saudi is paid $13,400 a year. The people of Bangladesh have the lowest income. Their average income is $117 a year.

15

FAMILY LIFE

All over the world there are people living in family groups, large and small. All families are similar in some ways — the members of the family share a home and a way of life. They are related to each other and depend on each other for love and support. They have rules and customs to help them live together happily.

Small families have perhaps a mother, a father, and one or two children. This is often called the "nuclear family." There are many one parent families, too.

Small families tend to be found in developed, wealthy parts of the world, such as Western Europe and North America. In these countries people often move away from their home, and sometimes live a long way from their own family and relatives.

In some countries families are traditionally large, with parents, children, and grandchildren all living near to each other or together in the same house. This is often called an "extended family."

Italy is an example of a country where there are lots of extended families. The parents and children may live on one floor of a house, with the grandparents of the family living on another.

Families in China have been encouraged to stay small by law. Some years ago the government decided to create a law that each family should have only one child.

The law stated that parents who decided to have more than one child could be punished by having their allowances of food and money reduced. These measures soon slowed down China's population growth.

Some houses are big enough for many families to live in. For example, the houses of the Dayak people of Borneo are so big that they are called longhouses.

One Dayak longhouse may make up a whole village, with as many as fifty families living together inside. These families share all the chores, possessions, and food.

Borneo longhouse

A kibbutz is a unique kind of home for some families in Israel. It is a large farm where all the people work and live together. The adults work on the farm during the day and the children go to a kibbutz school.

Everyone eats together in a big dining room, and the children sleep in one building, while the adults sleep in another. Even the babies have their own house to sleep in.

Kibbutz farm

LEISURE

Now that machines do so much work, people have more free time than ever before.

Throughout most of Europe and North America the most popular pastime is watching TV.

In these areas, nearly every family owns at least one TV set, and on average, people spend at least two hours each day watching it.

Other popular pastimes are reading, gardening, listening to music, and playing sports.

In warm countries, people tend to spend more of their free time outside. For example, in many Mediterranean countries families go out for walks together, or sit at cafés in the early evening.

Some of the most sociable people in the world are the islanders of the South Pacific, who spend nearly *all* their free time visiting each other's houses to eat, drink, and tell stories.

EDUCATION

Education is an important part of everyone's early life. What people learn helps them to think for themselves and lead useful lives.

Some children go to school to learn to read and write, using books and special school equipment. However, some children never go to school, but learn different skills instead. For example, in many African villages children learn how to hunt and make tools instead of how to read and write.

Today there are more schools in the world than ever before; but not all of them are in modern buildings with lots of teachers! For example, Indonesian schools are usually huts built from bamboo and reed, with long desks crowded with children. Children of all ages learn together in the same class.

In parts of Malaysia there are so many pupils that they have to go to school in two shifts!

The first shift begins lessons early in the morning and finishes at 1 o'clock. The second shift starts school at 1 o'clock and stays until the early evening.

Many children wear uniforms to show which school they go to. In warm countries the uniform may be a simple shirt worn with shorts or a skirt. In Argentina, children wear a white coat over their ordinary clothes.

In some places, such as Great Britain, uniforms are very formal — some schoolchildren must wear ties, jackets, and caps at all times. This type of uniform often carries the school badge.

School uniforms

School badge

In many countries children must go to school by law, but this is not always true. For instance, in poor parts of India children often have to work from an early age to earn money for their family. Millions of people cannot read and write because they have never been to school. More than half the populations of Africa, India, and the Caribbean have never learned these skills.

HOME AND AWAY

Not everyone is lucky enough to have a school nearby. Some children must travel a long way to attend classes. For instance, children who live on the far eastern coast of the Soviet Union come from homes which are very remote and isolated. They all must live away from home at boarding schools.

After classes they keep busy by dancing, singing, or doing sports. They also learn traditional skills at school, such as bone carving.

In some parts of Africa and Australia children stay at home — but they still attend school! They take part in a "school of the air," talking to their teachers over a two-way radio set. Their written work is usually sent by mail to be corrected.

Some children go to several different schools, all in the same term. They might do this if they are part of a gypsy family, traveling from town to town in parts of Europe, or if they live on a barge taking cargo up and down rivers and coasts in countries such as Holland and Germany. Wherever they stop, the children go to the nearest school.

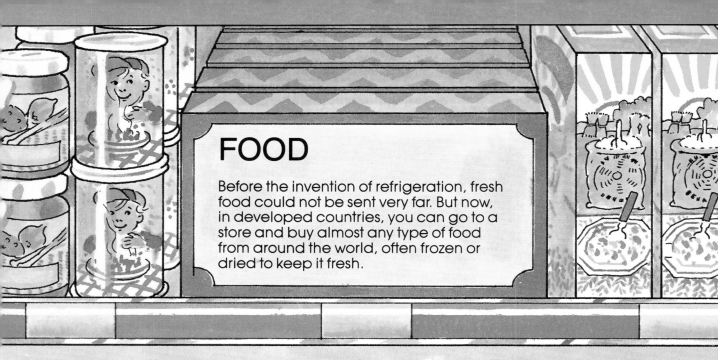

FOOD

Before the invention of refrigeration, fresh food could not be sent very far. But now, in developed countries, you can go to a store and buy almost any type of food from around the world, often frozen or dried to keep it fresh.

Prehistoric people gathered plant food and hunted for animals in the countryside around them. In some parts of the world tribes still live in this way, especially in Africa. They are called hunter-gatherers.

In developing countries, bad weather or war can destroy food supplies and cause famine. International organizations such as the UN are working to try to prevent this from happening (see p. 42).

The Kalahari bushmen of southern Africa are hunter-gatherers who live in a dry desert region. They know where to dig for bulbs and tubers (buried roots) hidden in the ground. These provide some food and water when other supplies are hard to find.

Tubers

The Japanese Puffer fish has a poisonous sac which has to be removed by trained chefs. It is thought that up to 200 people a year die from eating it.

The Australian Aborigines sometimes go hunting for food in the barren Outback. Their delicacies include wombat, kangaroo, lizard, and the witchetty grub, the giant larva of an Australian beetle.

In some parts of Kenya, after rain showers, the air is filled with flying white ants.
Local children like to gather the ants and take them home to fry in butter and eat. They are said to taste like nuts.

In Britain, plum pudding is soaked in brandy and set on fire at Christmas. The flaming pudding signals that winter will soon end and the sun will return.

FAMILY LIFE FACTFINDER

A school education is now required in many countries throughout the world. The first country to introduce this was Prussia (now part of Germany) in 1819.

The biggest school in the world is South Point High School in Calcutta, India. It has more than 12,000 pupils.
The university with the most students is the State University of New York, which has over 150,000 students.

Milk is one of the most important foods in the world, much of it coming from cows. However, Indians and Chinese drink the milk of water buffaloes and the Lapps of northern Europe drink the milk of wild reindeer. Mongolians drink horses' milk, Tibetans drink yaks' milk, and many Arabs drink camels' milk.

The black truffle of Perigord, in France, is just a small, wrinkled fungus which grows underground. But it is the most expensive food in the world, selling for around $30 an ounce.

Many kinds of food have traveled a long way from their original homes. For instance, domestic chickens, potatoes, and sweet corn all originated in South America. Yams were brought to the West Indies by slaves from West Africa, and carrots originally came from western Asia.

The largest families in the world are probably the tribal groups of central Africa. In Ghana, the Ashanti live in big square houses with an open yard in the center. Dozens of children may live in one house with their sisters, mothers, and aunts. Their fathers live in another house — with THEIR mothers and brothers and sisters!

A peasant woman who lived two hundred years ago near Moscow, in Russia, is said to have had 69 children. It is recorded that she gave birth to several sets of twins, triplets, and quadruplets, as well as many single babies.

LANGUAGE & CUSTOMS

If you traveled around the world you would come across many different languages and everyday customs. For instance, on your journey you would see people wearing different types of clothes, playing different sports and games, and celebrating all kinds of different traditional festivals. Some of the variations are explained in this section.

LANGUAGES

There are approximately 4,000 different world languages. Chinese is the most widely used, spoken by 1 billion people. There are many different forms of Chinese; in the north of China people speak Mandarin, while those in the south mostly speak Cantonese.

English is the second most widely spoken language. About 350 million people use it throughout the world. After that comes Hindi (an Indian language) with 145 million, Russian with 130 million, Spanish with 125 million, and German with 120 million.

Most languages have some words which were originally borrowed from other sources. For instance, words in many European languages are based on ancient Latin, spread by the Romans when they colonized new areas. There are also words based on ancient Greek and even some words borrowed from Arabic and Indian speech.

People who learn Latin and Greek have a head start in learning other languages, because many of the words are very similar.

The Arctic Inuit (also called Eskimos) have one of the world's most descriptive languages. For example, whereas in English there is only one word for "snow," the Inuit have at least six words describing different types of snow.

"Non-kot-za" means snow on the ground. "Seth-che" means windblown snow. "They-ni-zee" means powdery snow. "Za-he-ah-tree" means drifting snow. "Det-thlok" means snow deep enough for snowshoes, and "Za-kay-tak-lok" means long-lasting snow!

In southern Africa many tribes use "click" sounds when they talk. Among these are the Zulus, the Bushmen, and the Xhosa.

There are several different kinds of "click," each meaning something different. Some are made at the back of the throat, some with the side of the tongue, and some between the front teeth.

Another unusual way of speaking is the whistle language used by a tribe of Mexican Indians. They have a variety of whistles which can mean everything they want.

NEW LANGUAGES

World languages are changing all the time, as new words are invented and old ones forgotten. Sometimes whole new languages develop.

Creole is a relatively new language. It is spoken by many people in the Caribbean, and is a mixture of Dutch, English, Spanish, and African. It developed when European traders sailed to the region, bringing African slaves.

Sign language was developed for deaf people. It uses hand signs for letters and words.

The Braille language for blind people was developed by Frenchman Louis Braille, himself blind. While he was still a student, Louis developed the Braille system of raised dots punched on paper. Each alphabet letter has its own raised dot pattern, which you can feel with your fingers.

A century ago, a Polish professor invented a new language called Esperanto. It was made up from several European languages, and the professor hoped that it would become a universal language, spoken by everyone throughout the world. But today there are only about 100,000 Esperanto speakers.

Pidgin English is a form of simple English invented by early traders; it is still spoken in Pacific island areas. A typical example is the phrase for "piano," which is "big bokkus (box) time you fight him he cry out."

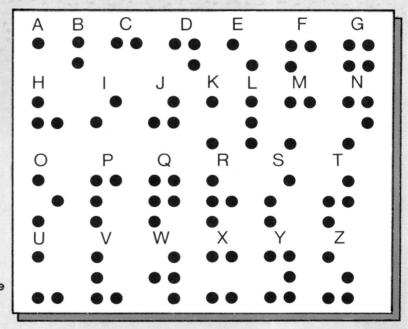

The braille language

COUNTING ROUND THE WORLD

Here are the words for "one, two, three" in several languages.

English: one, two, three
German: eins, zwei, drei
Italian: uno, due, tre
Russian: ahdeen, divah, tree
Chinese: ee, ur, san
Hindi (Indian): ayk, do, teen
Ashanti (African): eko, ena, esa

CLOTHES

Clothes are an important part of everyday life. Some types of clothing are useful, for example, to keep people warm or dry.

Some clothes are traditional, for example, the Indian sari. However, some clothes are worn simply because they are fashionable.

Cave paintings show prehistoric people hunting creatures such as antelope. They probably made the first clothes out of the animal skins.

Animal skins are still used today for leather shoes, belts, and coats.

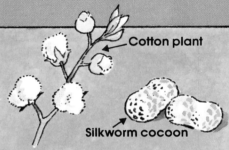

Cotton plant

Silkworm cocoon

Cotton is a natural fiber used for clothing. It comes from the fluffy fibers that surround the seeds of the cotton plant. These are spun and woven into fabric.

Silk is a silvery thread made by caterpillars called silkworms. The caterpillars live on mulberry trees, which are specially cultivated on silk farms.

For centuries animal hair has been used to make clothes. The woolly fleece of sheep is cut off once a year and the fibers are spun into wool. Goat, camel, and even rabbit hair is used in the same way.

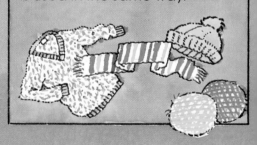

KEEPING WARM

In cold places such as the Arctic, it is vital to wear warm clothes because they could save your life.

The traditional clothes of the Arctic Inuit include thick pants made of seal or reindeer skin, thick skin gloves, jackets trimmed with wolf fur, and strong seal skin boots stuffed with dry grass.

The best way to keep warm is to wear several layers of clothing. Air is trapped between the layers and helps warm the body.

TRADITIONAL CLOTHES

Many countries have traditional costumes which have been worn for hundreds of years. They are often worn at special occasions such as festivals and international events.

One of the richest-looking traditional costumes is the Malaysian wedding gown, made from "cloth of gold," which is woven from silk and embroidered with gold thread.

UNIFORMS

Many people wear uniforms to show that they are part of a group. For instance, policemen, soldiers, nurses, and fire fighters usually wear uniforms, although the type of clothes vary from country to country.

Police uniforms are a good example of how uniforms vary. In many countries policemen wear shirts, pants, and caps, but a Fijian policeman may wear a shirt, a pair of sandals, and a skirt called a sulu.

KEEPING COOL

In some hot areas people wear no clothes, but a different way of keeping cool is to wear loose clothes covering the whole body. For instance, the Tuareg tribesmen of the Sahara wear long robes which shield them from the sun but let air flow freely around their bodies.

GAMES AND SPORTS

There are hundreds of different sports and games. Some of them are played all over the world, whereas others are traditional local games which have never spread beyond the country where they were first invented.

Soccer

American football

Soccer is probably the most popular sport in the world. It was first played in China over 2,000 years ago, and now almost every country has a national team.

Several games have grown out of soccer. In rugby football and American football players play with an oval ball. In Australian football the ball can be punched, bounced or kicked.

The Iroquois Indians of North America play a winter sport called snowsnakes. The spear "snakes" can reach speeds of 120 mph and travel well over a mile.

In Acapulco, Mexico, high diving from a cliff is a popular sport. Divers jump 115 feet into 13 feet of water. Months of practice are needed to avoid injury.

The fastest sport in the world is probably jai alai, or pelota, which is similar to racquetball. Players wear a large scoop-shaped racket on one hand. The idea is to hit a rubber ball against three walls.

NATIONAL GAMES

The traditional sport of Japan is sumo wrestling. The wrestlers must train hard for many years and they must also eat hard! The aim of the fight is to force your opponent to the ground or out of the ring. Sumo wrestlers are very heavy — most of them weigh over 280 pounds!

A type of hockey on horseback, called polo, is played by people in Argentina, India, and Great Britain. The players use long sticks with mallet heads to hit a solid wooden ball around the field.

Polo grounds are huge, measuring over 300 yards long and 200 yards wide.

The national game of Canada is ice hockey, which was first played on the country's frozen lakes and harbors.

Each team has six players, who are well-padded for protection. The idea is to try to flick a puck into the goal with sticks.

OLYMPIC GAMES

The Olympic Games, held every four years, are open to athletes from every nation. The Games were revived in 1894, on the model of ancient Greek games held at Olympia.

At the Games opening ceremony all the participants parade in the stadium, and the Olympic flame is lit. The flame is carried by a relay of runners all the way from Olympia, and it burns throughout the Games.

FESTIVALS

Just about every day of the year is a special one somewhere in the world. There are many different festivals, holidays, and celebrations. Here are a few of them:

January 26th: Australia Day
Australians celebrate the day on which the first fleet of ships, carrying English convicts, landed in 1788.

February 2nd: Tu B'Shevat
In Israel, many children go out and plant trees on this day — cedars for boys and cypresses for girls.

March 3rd: Dolls' Festival
A special set of dolls is put on display in Japanese homes. The dolls are offered gifts of food and drink.

April: The Death of Winter
Czechoslovakian children burn straw effigies decorated with rags and eggshells which represent winter.

May 1st: May Day Parade
In the Soviet Union, thousands of people parade through Moscow's Red Square, carrying banners, posters, and flags.

June 21st: Midsummer's Day
In England, priests of the ancient druid religion celebrate midsummer at the Stonehenge stone circle.

July 4th: American Independence Day The people of the U.S. hold parties to celebrate the day they became independent from Britain in 1776.

September: Chinese Moon Festival The Chinese celebrate the birthday of the moon by exchanging specially decorated cakes and toy pagodas.

October: Diwali, the Festival of Lights The first day of the Hindu New Year in India. Thousands of lamps are lit on this day to welcome the Hindu goddess Lakshmi.

CUSTOMS FACTFINDER

The most expensive clothes ever made are the space suits worn by the crew of the space shuttle for work outside their spacecraft. These suits cost over 2 million dollars to make. The most expensive dress ever was made in Paris in 1977. It was an evening gown decorated with over 500 diamonds. It was priced at over 1 million dollars!

The earliest written language is Chinese, which is more than 6,000 years old. It also has the longest alphabet, with about 20 million different symbols. The most complex of them is the character meaning "talkative," which takes 64 pen strokes to write!

The most expensive cloth ever made was called "shatoosh." It was woven from the gray throat hairs of Indian goats, and sold for $1,000 a yard. It is impossible to buy now.

The world's biggest carnival is held in Rio de Janeiro, Brazil, famous for its statue of Christ on a clifftop. "Carnival" comes from a Latin phrase meaning "meat farewell," referring to the fasting for Lent which begins on the Wednesday when Carnival ends.

The most widely-played sport in the world is thought to be soccer. The biggest soccer stadium in the world is in Rio de Janeiro in Brazil. This stadium can hold over 205,000 people.

The oldest printed language work ever found is a scroll made from wooden printing blocks. It was discovered in the foundations of a pagoda in South Korea, and it is thought to be over 1,000 years old.

The fastest of all sports is sky diving (jumping from an airplane and falling freely before releasing your parachute). The fastest falling speeds occur at high altitudes, where the air is thinnest. Some sky divers have been clocked at speeds of over 620 miles per hour!

The toughest of all sporting events must be the Iron Man Triathlon held in Hawaii. The contestants first swim 2.4 miles, then bicycle 112 miles and finally run a marathon of 26 miles.

29

ART AND MUSIC

Each country in the world has its own traditional forms of art, music, dance, and handicrafts. These types of skills are often centuries old and have been handed down from generation to generation.

In many areas books, plays, and movies also play an important part in artistic life.

PAINTING

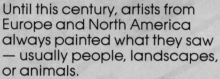

Until this century, artists from Europe and North America always painted what they saw — usually people, landscapes, or animals.

However, many modern artists now paint "abstract" works, using patterns, splashes, and whirls of color to try to create exciting effects.

Some tribal artists paint or tattoo their own bodies. For instance, the Australian Aborigines paint their bodies with red and white decorations for special ceremonies.

The Andaman Islanders of the Indian Ocean cover their entire bodies with tiny scars to form complex patterns.

The walls of houses are sometimes used as surfaces for painted pictures. For instance, in southern Africa the people of the Ndebele tribe build their mud huts with rounded walls and high arches. Then they decorate all the walls with strong, brightly-colored patterns.

MUSICAL INSTRUMENTS

The earliest instruments were probably drums and gongs, which were hit to make simple sounds. Today all kinds of different instruments can be heard around the world.

Gamelan orchestras, from Indonesia and Thailand, combine all kinds of gongs, drums, bells, and xylophones. They play for religious ceremonies, dancing, and puppet plays.

Gamelan instruments

Steel band

Indian sitar

A symphony orchestra

In the West Indies, musicians make their own instruments out of oil drums. The tops of the drums are carefully tuned to play different notes when they are hit.

The most important instrument in Indian music is the sitar, which has a long neck and twenty strings. When it is played it makes a distinct wavering sound.

A modern symphony orchestra has between 90 and 120 members. About half of these play string instruments.

DANCES

Dancing is part of many festivals and events. Some dances are traditionally performed at certain times. For instance, during the month of May, English children can sometimes be seen dancing around a maypole to welcome the spring.

Tribal dances often represent such things as battles, animals, and gods. For instance, the Watusi people of central Africa dance in two long lines, dressed for battle. The herdsmen of Mongolia have wild dances in which they imitate horses galloping over the plains.

The exciting Spanish flamenco is a world-famous local dance, probably first devised by gypsies.
  In a flamenco the men stamp their heels and toes and the women make graceful hand and body movements, wearing brightly-colored costumes with swirling skirts.

BOOKS AND PLAYS

People have always enjoyed listening to stories. Before the development of writing, storytellers often wandered through countries telling traditional tales of gods, heroes, and great events.

There are still many such storytellers today. In China, they are paid to go from school to school to tell ancient tales. In many African tribes, the storyteller is an important and respected person.

When the printing press was invented about five centuries ago, people began to get their stories from books. Today thousands of books are published around the world each year.

You can buy books or borrow them from libraries. Almost every big city in the world has a library where, in addition to books, manuscripts, records, diaries, and other documents are often kept. The largest library of this kind is the U.S. Library of Congress, which contains nearly 80 million different items!

THEATERS

Greek theater

Kabuki actor

The original Globe theater.

The first theaters were built in ancient Greece. They had semicircular open-air stages with rows of stone seats for the audience. There are still some Greek theater ruins to be seen, and some modern theaters are built on this model.

In Japan, traditional Kabuki plays are popular. They are performed on a wide revolving stage and all the parts are played by men. All the actors wear embroidered costumes and elaborate makeup on their faces.

There is a theater especially built for plays by William Shakespeare (1564–1616) in Stratford-on-Avon, England. However, the Canadian town of Stratford has built a copy of the Globe theater, where the plays were first performed.

MOVIES

Movies are made in many countries, but the center of the movie world is still the town of Hollywood, in California. The major movie studios are there and many famous movie stars live nearby in Beverly Hills.

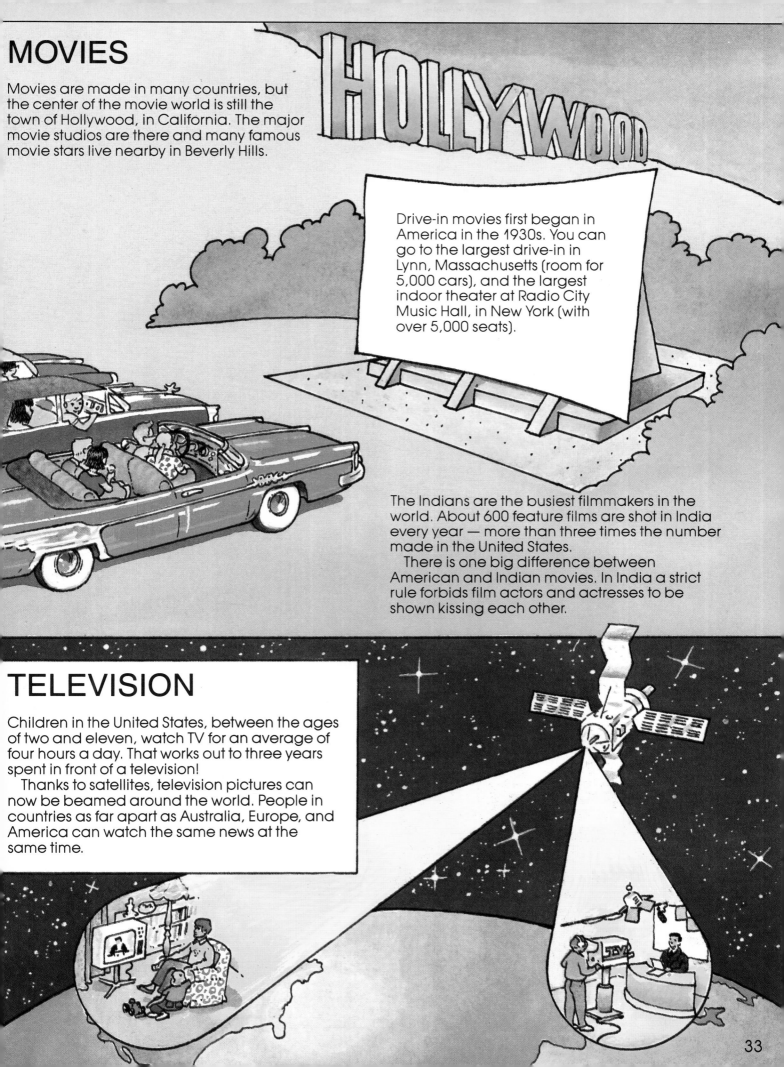

Drive-in movies first began in America in the 1930s. You can go to the largest drive-in in Lynn, Massachusetts (room for 5,000 cars), and the largest indoor theater at Radio City Music Hall, in New York (with over 5,000 seats).

The Indians are the busiest filmmakers in the world. About 600 feature films are shot in India every year — more than three times the number made in the United States.

There is one big difference between American and Indian movies. In India a strict rule forbids film actors and actresses to be shown kissing each other.

TELEVISION

Children in the United States, between the ages of two and eleven, watch TV for an average of four hours a day. That works out to three years spent in front of a television!

Thanks to satellites, television pictures can now be beamed around the world. People in countries as far apart as Australia, Europe, and America can watch the same news at the same time.

33

WORLD CRAFTS

Before there were machines, nearly everything that was worn or used in the home had to be made by hand (by "craft"). There are still many craft workers throughout the world.

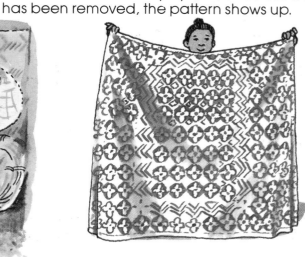
Tartan loom

CLOTH MAKERS

The world-famous Scottish tartan, used for kilts, is still woven on hand-operated looms. Different Scottish families (or "clans") have their own traditional tartan patterns. Over 13,000 patterns are recorded.

The people of the Pacific Islands use the leaves from trees to weave many household items, such as mats, baskets, hats, and fans. The children are taught to weave in school.

A special kind of cloth called batik has been produced in Java, Indonesia, for centuries. A pattern is painted on the cloth with wax, and the cloth is then dyed. The areas covered by wax do not receive any dye, so, once the wax has been removed, the pattern shows up.

Batik pattern

CARVERS

Soapstone carving

Every man in the Kenyan Kisii tribe learns to be a craftsman. The Kisii use soapstone from nearby quarries, carving it into figures of people and animals. They sell the carvings to tourists and other tribespeople.

Skilled Chinese craftspeople have made ivory carvings for centuries. It takes years to learn the skill, and the carvers are able to make some astonishingly intricate carvings with lots of tiny detail.

In Nigeria there are wood-carvers who make special masks for religious festivals. They also carve figures of gods and warriors for the shrines of the local Epa religion, in which the god of wood is worshipped.

Wooden mask

Ivory carving

ART AND CRAFTS FACTFINDER

The Statue of Liberty, which stands at the entrance to New York harbor, is probably the best-known and certainly the largest statue in the world. It stands on a base made of granite and concrete, and is made of copper sheets over a steel framework. The statue is 305 feet tall from tip to base.

The largest band of all time was assembled in Oslo, Norway in 1964. It was made up of 20,000 band members from all over the country.

Tapestry is a very old craft, still practiced today. Some fragments of tapestry were found in the tomb of an ancient Egyptian pharaoh over 3,000 years old.

The largest and loudest of all musical instruments is the organ built in Atlantic City, New Jersey, in 1930. It has 33,000 pipes and can play as loudly as 25 bands! Its loudest stop (musical note) is 6 times noisier than the loudest train whistle there is.

The Bible, which has been translated into many languages, is thought to be the best-selling book ever. No one knows how many million copies have been sold through the centuries.

The oldest known works of art are some blocks of stone carved with figures of animals and women. They were found in Perigord, in France, and are thought to be over 25,000 years old.

Persian carpets are woven by hand (see p. 13). They are among the most expensive craft objects you can buy.

The most costly carpet ever made was woven from gold thread and sewn with emeralds. It was produced for a palace in Iraq, but was later cut up by looters.

The first full-length book to be printed was the Bible. It was produced on a printing press by Johann Gutenberg in Mainz, Germany in 1454.

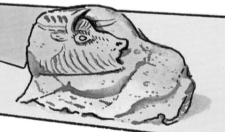

WORLD RELIGION

A religion is a set of beliefs about life and the way that people should live. Most religions also teach people to worship a god and to love and respect each other. Many millions of people throughout the world follow the religions explained in this section.

BUDDHISM

Buddhist shrine

Over 2,500 years ago, an Indian prince set out to discover the reasons why there was suffering in the world.

The prince decided that pain and suffering were caused by human greed, and that if people could stop being greedy their suffering would also stop and they would gain inner peace by meditation.

After his death the prince was known as the Buddha.

There are now over 250 million people following the teachings of Buddha. Most of them live in countries such as India, Nepal, Tibet, Malaysia, Burma, and Thailand.

Buddhists try to live a simple life. They do not eat meat or drink alcohol. They make daily visits to temples, where they place flowers and lighted candles before a statue of the Buddha.

JUDAISM

Judaism was founded by Abraham, the leader of the Jewish people. He taught the Jews to worship and obey one supreme God. Today there are about 14 million Jews, most of them living in the U.S., Europe, the USSR, and Israel.

Saturday is the Jewish day of prayer and rest from work. On this day Jews attend services in synagogues and read from the Jewish holy books, the Torah and the Talmud. The most important Jewish festival is Yom Kippur, when Jews ask God's forgiveness for wrongs they may have done.

Inside a synagogue

HINDUISM

Hinduism is the main religion of Indian communities, with over 500 million believers.

A Hindu Brahmin

Representations of Hindu gods

Hindus believe that when people die they return to earth in new forms. If someone has lived a wicked life they will come back as a lower animal, such as an insect or a snake.

Only good and holy people will be released from the cycle of life, death, and rebirth.

Hindus worship many gods. The chief of these is Brahma, the creator of all things. Other important gods are the gentle Vishnu who preserves life, and the fierce Shiva, who destroys it. Most Hindu homes have shrines with statues or pictures of these gods.

Hindus are divided strictly into five different classes, or castes. At the top are the priests, called "Brahmins." Next come rulers and warriors, then traders and craftsmen, and then ordinary workers. The fifth group, the "Untouchables," do the dirty and unpleasant jobs.

CHRISTIANITY

The Christian religion was founded 2,000 years ago by Jesus, who Christians believe is the son of God who came to earth to save people from sin. His disciples spread Christianity throughout the world, and today there over 1,200 million Christian followers.

Christians believe that Jesus was put to death on a cross, but rose again. The cross is the symbol of Christianity.

Sunday is the Christians' holy day, when they go to church to worship God. The major Christian churches are called cathedrals.

The Pope

Archbishop

There are several different Christian groups. For example, the Catholic Church, based in Rome, is led by the Pope. Some of the Protestant churches are led by archbishops.

ISLAM

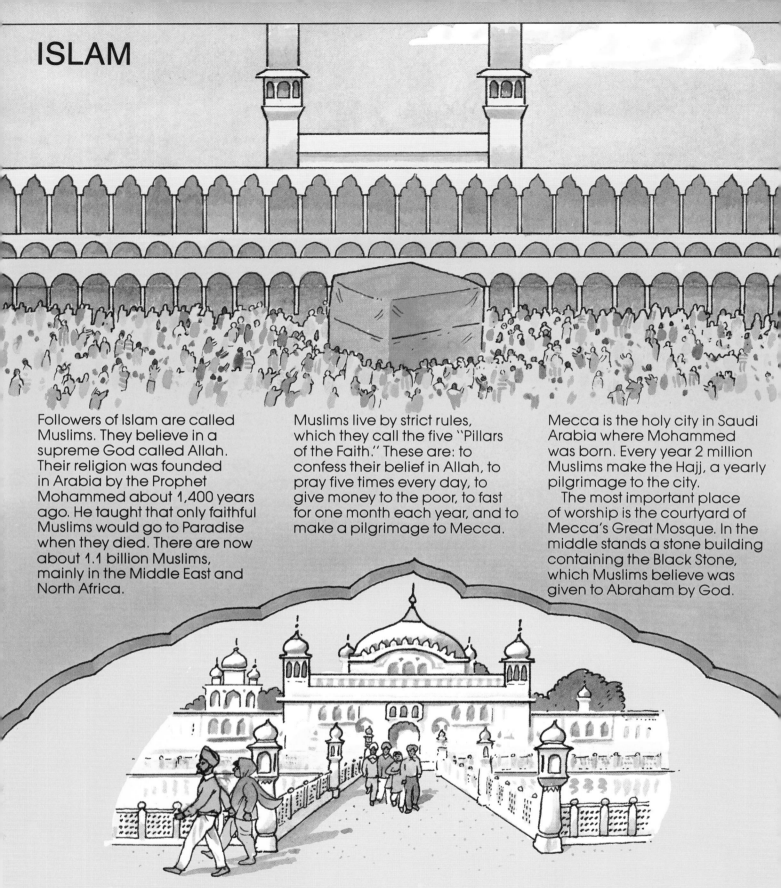

Followers of Islam are called Muslims. They believe in a supreme God called Allah. Their religion was founded in Arabia by the Prophet Mohammed about 1,400 years ago. He taught that only faithful Muslims would go to Paradise when they died. There are now about 1.1 billion Muslims, mainly in the Middle East and North Africa.

Muslims live by strict rules, which they call the five "Pillars of the Faith." These are: to confess their belief in Allah, to pray five times every day, to give money to the poor, to fast for one month each year, and to make a pilgrimage to Mecca.

Mecca is the holy city in Saudi Arabia where Mohammed was born. Every year 2 million Muslims make the Hajj, a yearly pilgrimage to the city.

The most important place of worship is the courtyard of Mecca's Great Mosque. In the middle stands a stone building containing the Black Stone, which Muslims believe was given to Abraham by God.

SIKHISM

Sikhism was founded in India about 500 years ago by Guru Nanak. It combines many of the ideas from the Hindu and Muslim faiths, such as belief in rebirth after death.

There are about 14 million followers of the religion, most of them coming from the Punjab region of India.

Sikh men believe themselves to be part of a chosen race of warrior-saints. They follow five strict rules of appearance (called the "Five Ks"). They must not cut their hair or shave, they must keep a comb in their hair, wear shorts under their pants, wear a steel bracelet, and carry a short dagger.

RELIGION FACTFINDER

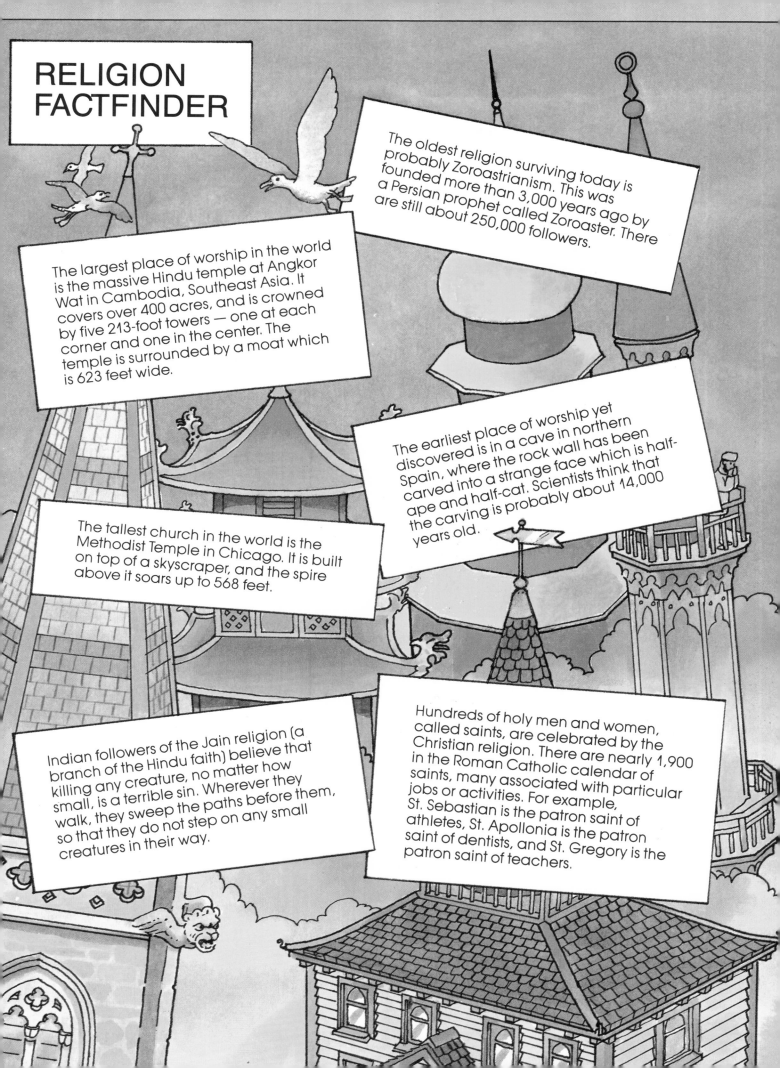

The oldest religion surviving today is probably Zoroastrianism. This was founded more than 3,000 years ago by a Persian prophet called Zoroaster. There are still about 250,000 followers.

The largest place of worship in the world is the massive Hindu temple at Angkor Wat in Cambodia, Southeast Asia. It covers over 400 acres, and is crowned by five 213-foot towers — one at each corner and one in the center. The temple is surrounded by a moat which is 623 feet wide.

The earliest place of worship yet discovered is in a cave in northern Spain, where the rock wall has been carved into a strange face which is half-ape and half-cat. Scientists think that the carving is probably about 14,000 years old.

The tallest church in the world is the Methodist Temple in Chicago. It is built on top of a skyscraper, and the spire above it soars up to 568 feet.

Indian followers of the Jain religion (a branch of the Hindu faith) believe that killing any creature, no matter how small, is a terrible sin. Wherever they walk, they sweep the paths before them, so that they do not step on any small creatures in their way.

Hundreds of holy men and women, called saints, are celebrated by the Christian religion. There are nearly 1,900 in the Roman Catholic calendar of saints, many associated with particular jobs or activities. For example, St. Sebastian is the patron saint of athletes, St. Apollonia is the patron saint of dentists, and St. Gregory is the patron saint of teachers.

POLITICS AND LAW

A small tribe may be made up of fewer than a hundred people, whereas a large country may contain many millions; however, both societies need rules to help their people live together in peace. In most countries the rules are set and enforced by a group of officials called a government.

RULERS

Heads of American presidents carved on Mount Rushmore.

Some countries are ruled by one person who must be obeyed in all things. Such rulers are called dictators.

The British monarch is an example of a ruler without power. The British Parliament makes the laws.

The American and French heads of state are presidents. They exercise power, but work with elected representatives.

Small groups with their own language and customs are called tribes. They, too, must have laws in order to survive successfully. For instance, in the South American Amazon, the jungle tribes organize themselves in different ways. Some tribes have a headman and a council of elders, while in other groups every member has equal rights and all possessions are shared.

In communist countries the laws are made and enforced by the communist party through committees of members. In Russia the most powerful committee is called the Politbureau.

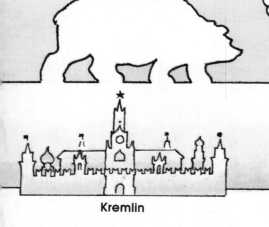

Kremlin

White House

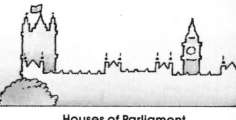

Houses of Parliament

Many governments have a central building where important decisions are made. The Kremlin in Moscow is the home of Russian government.

The American president lives in the White House, in Washington, D.C. This mansion has become a world-renowned symbol of American government.

The houses of Parliament in London are the home of the British government. The famous clock tower, Big Ben, is part of the building.

VOTING

In democratic countries regular elections are held in which citizens can vote for someone to represent them in government.

Voters often have a choice of political parties, groups who hold particular views and promise to put them into action once elected.

Presidents are sometimes elected, too. For example, the American president is elected by U.S. citizens every four years.

Through democratic elections, a country's voters can choose new governments. However, in communist countries voters have only one party to vote for, so after every election the same government is in power.

LAW AND ORDER

In most countries there is a "judicial system" to try criminal suspects and sentence those found guilty.

In many trials a "jury" of individuals helps to decide on the evidence. This custom began in ancient times, and has spread all over the world.

Usually a judge, who is a trained lawyer, presides over a court and directs the proceedings. In 18th century Britain the judges wore horsehair wigs and long gowns. This tradition still remains and has been followed in many other countries.

Every country has its own police force to make sure that its laws are obeyed.

One of the world's most famous police forces is the Canadian Mounted Police, known as the "Mounties." However, today they rarely go on patrol on horseback and usually travel by car. They only wear their famous red coats and broad-brimmed hats on special occasions.

Most countries have prisons for those found guilty of crime. The most secure prison ever was Alcatraz Island, in San Francisco Bay. No one ever escaped successfully.

THE UNITED NATIONS

The UN flag →

Countries have often made alliances, forming groups for trade or even war. Today there are several trading groups, but the biggest and most important grouping of countries is the United Nations, based in New York City.

Every member country has a vote in the UN General Assembly, where world issues are debated. There is also a Security Council of 15 countries, which have the final say on United Nations policy.

The UN organizes several groups to look after different issues. For instance, it runs the International Court of Justice at the Hague, in Holland. In this court governments can be brought to trial for unfair or violent acts. The World Health Organization (WHO) works to combat diseases, and the UN Children's Fund (UNICEF) works to help the children of the world.

The United Nations flag shows a world map circled by olive branches, symbols of peace.

NATIONAL FLAGS

Every country has its own flag. Some examples are shown below.

Italy   France   Britain   U.S.A.   Australia   Brazil   Canada   Japan   China

Many flags are based on historic traditions; for instance, the Italian flag is based on the colors of the flag used by Napoleon when he invaded Italy in 1796. The French tricolor is based on red and blue, the colors of Paris, plus white, which represents French Royalty.

Some flags show emblems from different regions. For instance, the British flag combines the English, Scottish, and Irish emblems.

Some flags show symbols of their country. For instance, the Canadian flag shows a Canadian maple leaf, and the Japanese flag shows the sun. The Japanese call their country "Nippon," meaning "source of the sun."

The Russian flag has a hammer and sickle, representing Russian factory and farm workers. The Chinese flag has five stars representing five types of Chinese worker.

Some countries have star patterned flags. The Australian flag has one seven-pointed star representing seven districts, and five stars showing the Southern Cross constellation.

The American flag has 50 stars for its 50 states and 13 stripes representing its original 13 colonies.

The Brazilian flag has 23 stars representing its states, arranged in the pattern of the night sky over Brazil.

GOVERNMENT FACTFINDER

The oldest known flag, from Iran, dates from 3000 B.C. It was made of metal and decorated with lions, goddesses, and an eagle.

The longest of all reigns was probably that of Musoma Kanijo, a tribal chief in part of Tanzania. He came to the throne in 1864 and died in 1963, reigning for 98 years.

The Emperor Minhti of Burma reigned for 95 years, from 1279 to 1374, and the Pharaoh Phiops of ancient Egypt reigned for 94 years between 2281 and 2187 B.C.

The oldest of all regular parliaments is the Court of Tynwald in the Isle of Man, U.K. It has been meeting for over 1,000 years.

The Althing Parliament of Iceland is a few years older, but it has not met regularly. It was abolished in 1800 and then restored in 1874.

From early times religious symbols have been used on flags. Christian countries have often used the cross symbol on their banners and flags, and Islamic countries use the Muslim crescent moon symbol as one of their flag emblems.

Examples of crescent flags include Turkey, Tunisia, and Pakistan.

Saudi Arabia is ruled by the Saud family. The king is advised by his ministers, many of whom are also members of the Saud family. In fact the family has over 4,000 members, so they are likely to rule for a long time.

In communist countries people often have only one party to vote for, so it is not surprising that in 1962 everybody in North Korea voted for the communist party, since there was no one else on the ballot! The same thing nearly happened in Albania in 1982. Everybody voted for the communists except one man, who ruined his ballot paper.

FUTURE WORLD

People's lives are rapidly changing, especially as new machinery is invented for use in the home and at work. In this final section you can find out how modern developments are going to affect everyone's lives, wherever they live in the world.

In America and Europe more and more people have their own satellite dishes and can get information very fast from all around the world.

Dishes will become more common in the future. That means that people may be able to watch all sorts of TV programs in many different languages.

Satellites are not just used for TV entertainment. In isolated parts of the world they are becoming increasingly useful. For instance, remote schools can use dishes to receive lessons via TV, and isolated villages can receive news and vital information.

In the future, people will be able to travel much more quickly around the world, as faster planes and trains are invented. One future development may be a very fast jet plane which scientists are working on at the moment. It will fly very high, almost in space, and it will have a much more streamlined shape than today's planes.

In the distant future space travel could become much more common. There are even plans for people to live in space colonies orbiting the earth. Inside the colonies there will be an artificial atmosphere, and it may even be possible to grow food for the colony people.

Not all technological developments are good news for our future. The world is being increasingly polluted by industrial waste and fumes, and another major problem is the cutting down of the world's rainforests. These vast jungles provide oxygen for the atmosphere, but they are being gradually cleared for timber. Some scientists think that this is affecting the world's climate.

Many people in the world are starving, yet there is plenty of food being produced. However, it is difficult to transport the food to the right places, or to predict when and where famines will occur. Scientists are trying to find ways of solving this problem in the future.

Because of better communications in the future we will all be able to learn a lot more about people's lives around the world. With improved transportation we are more likely to be able to travel to see different countries for ourselves. As our knowledge of the world increases perhaps we will understand each other better, and perhaps countries will be more likely to live in peace and harmony.

INDEX